Captive, Madeline Dyer's first poetry collection, is based on the therapy writings she produced when she was experiencing psychosis and OCD due to Autoimmune Basal Ganglia Encephalitis, a type of brain inflammation that causes neuropsychiatric symptoms. While her communication skills and cognitive abilities diminished due to the effects of the inflammation, she was able to share her thoughts and emotions via the written word, a process that gave her great comfort when she otherwise felt possessed.

Captive provides readers with a glimpse of her tormented mind during this dark time of loneliness, loss, and fear.

Autoimmune Basal Ganglia Encephalitis is a chronic condition, one Madeline is still battling against as she searches for doctors who can help her.

Other works by Madeline Dyer

FICTION

THE UNTAMED SERIES

Untamed
Fragmented
Divided
Destroyed

THE DANGEROUS ONES SERIES

A Dangerous Game
This Vicious Way

OTHER BOOKS

The Curse of the Winged Wight

CAPTIVE

A Poetry Collection
on OCD, Psychosis, and Brain Inflammation

Madeline Dyer

INEJA PRESS

Captive: A Poetry Collection on OCD, Psychosis, and Brain Inflammation

First edition, January 2020
Published by Ineja Press

Edited by Meg Eden
Cover Design by MatYan and Sarah Anderson Designs
Interior Design by Madeline Dyer

Print ISBN: 978-1-912369-13-3
eBook ISBN: 978-1-912369-12-6

The author can be contacted via email at Madeline@MadelineDyer.co.uk or through her website www.MadelineDyer.co.uk

I just want to get better
and see the stars
and believe in hope again

Contents

Captive

A Poetry Collection
on OCD, Psychosis, and Brain Inflammation

Looking Through Water

Tear-stained and bleary,
the shapes of the world
merge and the wrens
are flying,
too many of them
inside my head
scratching sand into my brain

and I want to escape it all
and swim up, up, up,
until my head breaks the surface
where the sun is warm
and the sky is blue
and the birds aren't out to get me
and my mind isn't broken.

But my eyes are heavy,
too heavy.
They weigh my mind down,
anchors from my skull,
and everything is too blurry
and I wake in the night
because I can't see
and my eyes are inside out.

Drowning and Melting

My feet are cold candles on the beach,
and my eyes are teapots,
and I see things I shouldn't see,
because my vision is twice and nothing is right
when the monster dances in my brain.

And why won't the doctors extinguish
the fire that burns my veins until the tubes wilt?
Because now I am drowning and melting
as I dance between worlds waving my flags,
trying to be noticed among all the crying girls.

The Night it all Began, It Started with Sand

In the beginning there was sand
and I think a lot of how it began
and I cannot forget
that night when Darkness spoke to me
in muted tones and soft words
laced with thunder and sand.

The despair that followed
was just a game to the monster
that Darkness planted inside my mind,
a game he could win so easily

and I remember those early days,
how the world wore sand
and there was so much sand
as the sharp voice of Darkness whispered:

Wake and you'll be different.
You won't know yourself.
And no one will know you.

I am fighting back, uncovering
myself from the gloomy shade

because I fell as Darkness spoke, marshy knees
breaking, because I was changing

and Darkness planted tall mirrors in my brain:
too big, too many faces, and I watched
their stems grow into haughty smiles
from haughty strangers who—

You won't like yourself
You won't have anyone
You'll only have me

—promised me the world
and gave nothing but the empty husks
of false pledges, sweet and deadly.

I cannot forget how the sand felt
gritty and rough and abrasive
as it held the blossoming nightmare,
rancid against my nose,
that was to become my life,
held it close around me,
bruising my skin
as the sand moved and how I fought as
each little grain
with life inside crawled over me

and the monster of Darkness
is shame, stuck to my arms, my face

and *get it off*

and I can't.

I'm not mad, I promise,
and the sand is real, and the grains are grinning,
a million teeth flashing,
and they are here to stay.

The Monster Often Manifests as OCD

and there is no pause
now I cannot turn my thoughts off
for they spiral and spiral
and my tears are heavy and suffocating
and the rocks on my face will not leave
because they have claimed me
and I am theirs now

and I hate the name, OCD: trivial
just about neatness
and it is not and it is me
and I *cry cry cry* because I did something wrong
and I do not know what to do
and I cannot think because the stones on my brain
are too heavy

and that is the worse
this time of fear and indecision
because it sucks up time
as I think of all the possibilities
and all the ways I could do one simple thing
when only one way is right

and the compulsion is angry
because I cannot follow its directions
and I cannot see its solution amid my madness
and whatever I do needs to be perfect
and my day is broken
and my week is ruined
and my chance at happiness has gone
and still it will not stop

I cannot go out
and I cannot see friends because I am lost in the trees
and I cannot touch my horses because they are bad
and my guinea pigs are crawling with darkness
so I collapse in the bathroom sink where I can taste
the stench of antibacterial soap
and the tackiness of hand sanitizer
and the warm glow of chemicals
and the embrace of bitter shame of obsession
that clings to the compulsion in my burning mouth
and makes its home inside my *cold cold cold* bones
wrapped in sticky skin
and dry skin
and my skin is bleeding
and it's not my skin

and twenty washes
and thirty washes
and forty washes
and it is never enough
and I cannot escape
not for long
when I am a magnet
who has to keep returning to the sink

and now a fist I cannot make
not without unleashing it all
and it is a pliable shell of my old life
only it is not so pliable now

and I am safe
and I am sick and scared and stupid as the birds fly

and the air is so bad
I cannot breathe it in
and it must not fill my lungs
and *it mustn't, it mustn't, it mustn't*

so I go to the doctor
a ten-minute slot to explain it all
and *this isn't so bad*
and you do not understand
and *no, you're not severe*
and I am trying to tell you
and *here are some antidepressants*
and this is going to work
and *take this leaflet for therapy*

but the voice in my head
says there is nothing wrong
and I know it is right because the doctors are bad
because they don't listen
and they want to treat the symptoms
and not the cause
and this *suddenly happened*
and they say it is not normal
but they treat it the same and they ignore
my sight and my pain
and my hands are bleeding again
and so everyone is bad
and they do not understand

and neither do I
and this is it forever
and there is no pause

Being Cold is Being Safe

It sounds silly
being scared of a jumper
my jumper
green and loved and worn
and a thousand times it has sat
on my arms
and protected me
in its cosy hug

but now I know better
I cannot wear the jumper
for it is bad
the baddest of them all

it cannot touch my skin
must not touch it
because if you zoom
in on its fibres
you will see what it hides

the stories of the places it's been
and the marks of the people
it's met and the darkness
of the world
the tang of fuels
and stenches of engines
the promise of fumes
that nothing can get rid of

that cannot be on my skin
because it will grow and take
and make me deliver the badness

it has absorbed
to everything I touch.

My Invisible Torture

There is a maze in each of my kidneys
and at the centre of each maze is a fire on the sand

a fire of loss and revenge and heat
a greedy fire that takes and takes

the searing mazes are invisible secrets
and people do not look for things they cannot see
not when four packets of antibiotics
should have been enough
would have been enough
have been enough to tame the fire
to put it out

and they say the flames have gone
but they are there
hidden oh so well in the maze
where no doctors will search any longer

so the fires spread and the blisters breed
and the burns extract my gasps
and the laboured beats of my heart.

Things People Say

What is wrong
come on
talk to me
I do not understand
you have got to tell me

we want to help you
this isn't you
why are you crying

what
but this does not make sense
it cannot be upsetting you

this is silly
just touch the door
this is ridiculous
you weren't like this before
so why are you now
do not cry

just stop crying
you are not a child
do not act like one

you are upsetting everyone
look what you are doing
is that what you want
just look at yourself
pathetic

Things I Want to Say

I do not understand what is happening
this is not me
and I need help
but I do not know what is wrong
only that this is too much
too much effort

and how can this be it

day after day
and it does not change
the world just moves faster
and I am drowning
in the sea no one can taste

but it has me
this monster
it is swallowing me
and I am crying

but my tears feed it
and my breaths
are the beat of its wings
for it is everywhere
and I am scared
and this is exhausting

and it promises to never let me go

Things My OCD Tells Me Every Day

Don't touch the world.
The world is bad.
Don't sit down.
Change your clothes—do it now!
No, you're too late.
You've done it wrong
and the badness has spread.
It's killing people, can't you see?

Take your jumper off first—

Don't you remember?
Jumpers are bad!
Why are you wearing a jumper?
Look at the fibres, the badness.
It's alive, can't you see?
It's squirming, writhing.

You're not even trying!
You're doing it all wrong.
Listen to me.
Listen to me or bad things will happen.
Listen to me and I'll keep you safe.

Give me your hands,
and I'll give you a future.

An hour? Satisfactory.
Two hours? Good.
Three hours? Better.

No! Don't cry.
If your hands are bleeding,
you're doing it right.
That's your reward. Proof.
You can't dispute it.

No, don't stop!
Don't get lazy.
Do it now.

They don't understand.
Don't listen to them.
They want you to fail.
Their reassurances are lies.
They don't care.

My darling, I'm all you have.
I don't lie to you.
I keep you safe.

Hunger

Too far, too much
hunger inside me,
but I can't eat.

This food is not meant for me.

Fingers around my arm.
Smaller, smaller, smaller.

The scales laugh
and I see them everywhere,
and I don't want to stand on
the scales because there's a picture
of sand on the surface that grins
and spits out numbers

but I do stand there
eventually.

And I scream and cry,
huddled in my mind,
as the monster eats me inside out
in his new form

and I can't eat that
and I shan't eat that
and I won't eat that

and *that* is *anything*
and I don't know why.

But hunger claws inside me,
sharp teeth, searching,
and the words are there,
and the voices are there,
and they won't go,
and neither will my hunger.

I Want My Old Self Back

And I still don't understand how it all happened,
so quickly, so fast, the sand the start of it all,
because this is not me,
and I want to be free and think again.
I want to run barefoot through the grass
without hearing the whispers,
and I want to sleep and dream of fun,
not darkness and missiles and bleeding beaks.
I want to be myself again,
to feel and live. To not have compulsions
and ruined days and strict voices I must obey
to keep the Bad Stuff away.
I want to believe I can return to my former self
even when the voices say it was a lie
and that it never happened, not like that,
because I didn't know the danger I was in
as I ran through the woods,
but I do now. And I should be grateful,
but I'm not, and the OCD knows this,
so it promises to try harder.

The Doctor's Dress

I can't remember her
what she said
or the words that fell
though I wrote them down after
for later
little notes on my phone
but I remember her dress

that hideous dress

green, with lemons
a stark contrast
too bright
a pattern that made me dizzy
when I stared at it
as she talked
and talked and talked

of emergency admissions and tests and scans
her words meant to scare
with the cold stethoscope against
my chest
my back
and the dress up close
lemons laughing
green leaves dancing

and I want to run and escape
I want to dance and be free
dance until I fall
deep into the chasm

of the earth
to be forgotten
dangerous
dizzy and dancing
just like her dress.

When I Can't Control the Monster

Crying under broken stars
screaming behind the sharp arrows
trembling under the weight of life
as the monster inside me rises
and tells me my horses are bad

and the monster is me
because it has my voice and I cannot control it
as it crawls out and invites its winged friends

pitter patter pitter patter

the monsters' voices won't stop
and the birds won't stop taunting me
and I can't stop

pitter patter pitter patter

sobbing over the sink
begging the mirror
shouting at the road
to let me go.

The Birds

They're flying round
and round me again
circling
as they work out their plan

the crafty little creatures
the monster's cronies
they think I don't see them
but I do

their eyes are on me
searing holes in my skin
as they decide the best way to attack
with sharp little beaks waiting to peck

peck, peck, peck

I squeeze my eyes shut
a rushing sound
digs out my ears
but it doesn't block out the birds' wings

flap, flap, flap

a mob of them
and I am under attack

I am cold
frozen
but the birds have contaminated
my jumpers, my clothes

just by being in the room

and I must not touch them
being cold is being safe
my favourite phrase
for I have to have something
I can hold onto
and they won't leave me alone

chirp, chirp, chirp

I whimper and cry
the birds—they're just always there
and I can't see them, but they're here
I know they are
it's my vision that's gone wrong
I can't trust my eyes
they're not showing me the world

I can't do this
it's too difficult
and my heart of lost dreams cries,
a purple mess where flesh surrounds
darkness,
and I want to claw it out,
every suffocating, sinewy tissue; all of it
out. The rescue is needed.

Too much and it will fall. I will fall.
The suit of armour, broken. Gone.
Leaving only me.
The rage. The repulsion. The hunger.
And I am exposed for all the bad
heartless wrens to hurt.

When I Can't Cope, I am Scared

Paper dolls watch me with snake eyes
at 5 A.M., and their venom is sweet
and I want a break, something, anything,
to take it away, to take me away
from the dark beating wings

before the monster returns, screaming,

but now he is here
and he is OCD and Darkness and Pain
and Worry and the Birds and the Insects

he is it all

and I cannot think, because he fills my head
with broken words and chainsaws and drills,
beating too fast and heavy under stony wings,
and it is too much not to follow his orders
for pain in my hands, broken skin, and crimson drops

from my heart, fleshy, raw,
beating, for now
under the scalpel in his hand

this is all I have,
the things the monster makes me think,
and none of it is real

but my ankles are bleeding as the paper dolls
watch, and it doesn't make sense

and I am screaming at ears that cannot hear
because I want to live
not just survive.

Men in White Coats

Always there, watching, waiting
those hideous skulls
in long white coats.
Always bad, always good.

Take me away and I will fall, collapse
into darkness.
and I don't want to go to a psych ward,
because the monster will keep me there
because then he wins.

But the men in white coats are here, watching,
waiting in my nightmares.

And has it happened? Am I there, at the ward?
Did my family send me away? Is this real?

No.
I am here, home, still.
And I cannot go there,
the air at the hospital is bad,
too many things to touch,
too much contamination.

I'll run away,
don't make me go
to a prison too white
with screams as loud as silence
and whispers that cut.

An Apology to the Ponies

Muted amber light and crisp air and a snowflake
floating in the field in front of equine eyes.
Oh, when will you fall?

My footprints are soft in the blanket
but this is not my place now
but it does not matter
because there are too many eyes and commands
and *why can't you just do this?*

Oh, beautiful souls. Gentle muzzles and voices
send breaths into the frozen air, mark
their existence, their place.

I want to belong.

I want to run my fingers through the ponies' winter
coats, soft, warm, safe, hug them close.

I want to hug my family.

I want comfort as I stand in this slushy world
and try to breathe.

But I can't have what used to be mine.
The monster doesn't need to tell me
this time because his thoughts are mine
and mine are his,
irreparably entwined.

My stallion approaches, eyes

begging *please.*
A soft wicker. A neigh.

Voices, real. My mother, father.
Solid, here. Not a projection of my crushed mind.

Oh, you can do this,
we know you can.
And Victor wants a cuddle.

I shake my head. *Sorry.*

Eyes brim
and my heart snaps and the snowflake falls.

Spider, Spider, Insect, Bird

I am scared when I feel them,
when tiny feet patter on my flesh
in my muted world,
where days are grey, made of slush,
and I can't find my hammer.

They are bad, these spiders
and insects and birds, lacing dark poison
across my world, dirt only I can see,
and I must protect everyone from their venom.

But it is so much work,
and I need my hammer.
I need to crush the birds and insects
just as my mind has been crushed under stones,
because antidepressants haven't rescued
my inflamed brain.

And I am glad I can see them,
spider, spider, insect, bird,
in a way,
because now I know what else I need to clean
and avoid.

There's Nothing Wrong with You

He is a tall thin man and he smiles
as he tells me the results, as if it will please me
because there's nothing wrong and this is all in my head
and it's not a *real* problem, deserving of his time.

I don't like him, this doctor with the shiny suit
who makes me feel so small. But he has said it:
there's nothing wrong.

My kidneys *mustn't* be burning through life
because there are no boulders,
and my vision *must* be normal
because the neurologist said so with a smile
and a bemused look,
and my life *cannot* be hurting
because my bloods are within range,
the gunfire range,
and my scans are good and it's all in my head,
so why am I wasting his time?

Just talk to someone, he says,
but there's a waiting list and I am screaming
inside because he can't see what my life now is,
and I don't want it and I am possessed.

I see my soul, pink, inflamed, fleshy,
reduced to a watery, flat *nothing*
in the doctor's hands.
Hands that are supposed to care
but his hands are callous because his mind
is set and he's not willing to believe me

and research my symptoms to save me.

And I can't speak, and my words are bad
because I am not believed.
Too much saliva and not enough saliva
and sounds that stretch cobwebs over my head,
to try and fix what is clearly breaking.

And I am weak,
and his hands are my skull, the uncaring cage
around my captive, struggling mind.

But This Isn't Who I Am

I am not the girl who screams and screams
and wants to gouge out her eyes and write in blood
and run away and lose herself to the world.

I am not the girl who is scared of her family and friends
and who cannot bear to look at her animals
and who cannot watch TV without thinking
of all the contamination
the characters are exposed to.

Those crying girls have never been me.
I used to run and laugh and splash through mud
and play with my animals and go out with friends
and my mind would be quiet.

Now, I am deafened by the many voices in my head,
by this version of me who isn't me,
and I cannot see clearly, and I am drowning,
and why can't anyone hear my screams?

Captive

One lone tear slides
from its haven, reaching
out for something more.

Something better has to be there.

I catch that tear.
A pebble in my palm.
Proof of my pain and suffering.

The shadows are dark, my dearest
friend. And I want to let go, feel
the pounding rain on my skin.

I want to run and run and run,
find the smell of freshly cut grass
and feel a warm embrace.
But my walls are moving, silent.

A sanctuary. A prison. Captive.
I cannot move, only hold onto
my monster, my truest friend.

When I Go to the Medical Centre Again and Again and Again

Painted red lips watch as
patient #243352 checks in
and that is me

I am awkward
I am the person they warn you of
warn everyone of

for I am bad
and I can hear the receptionists whispering
and I see the notes on the doctors' screens

and I bring my family for backup
because I am not taken seriously
even by new doctors
as they have been primed on what to say

and all I want is help.

My Soul is Raw

I am not healing
because he never goes
he's there
my monster, with his cronies
spider, spider, insect, bird
but I never see him—the monster
just the idea of him, the feel of him,
that he could be there, watching,
and I will never know if I am free

let me go, let me be, let me live

but he gnashes his teeth and his jaws are too big
and darkness surrounds, and my flesh is raw
and there aren't enough words to bleed

help me, I whisper,
but now the voices are back, and they scream
an endless orchestra of pain, defeat, and cruelty
that drowns out my pleas.

The Beetle from My Mind

He watches me all the time,
the beetle with badly drawn eyes
and a tin-foil body stretched taut
over a pebble.

I see him a lot, I think, in my mind,
because he's how I envision my psychosis
because I don't want to be scared of it.
So I take the monster's underling and I shape him
into something cuter and friendlier
than the devil he is supposed to be.

Little legs and little arms.
A briefcase, glossy shoes, and a top hat.
A monocle, because he thinks it looks cool.
And he likes the Samba and Strictly,
so when I see him lurking in burning corners,
when the monster sends him to intimidate me,
I tell him to dance,
for he's in my mind, and that is my space.

My Hands

They are not mine, these hands,
they can't be because I do not recognise
the swollen, red fingers and the weakened skin
or the things these hands do

because I am a puppet for the monster,
and these hands have become his,
and he is a parasite, reaching
with long, sweet limbs
through my body, through my arms,
and he pulls the levers and my fingers obey,
deliver his words: shadows on the page, scrawling
and clumsy and it's not my handwriting
though everyone thinks I hold the pen

and he laughs as the ink floods,
as the shadows take what he offers.

I Can't Remember When Everything Happened

Everything happens at once,
and everything happened at once.
A tangled mesh that sits in my mind,
memories with no start and finish.

Recall it, they say. Make a timeline.
But there is no line.
It is a circle and it is a square
I cannot draw.
And it is bright and bland
and I can't remember the day we discovered
the brain inflammation, the day the real war began.

Everything and nothing,
Basal ganglia and frontal lobe and temporal lobe,
all at the same time, and I try to untangle it,
but my fingers are sticky
and the memories get stuck, stretched,
distorted.

But you must remember, they say.
When did this happen?

Time is broken inside my mind,
But they don't see it, feel it, live it, dream it.

Sometimes, I Get Really Good Days

Sometimes, I get really good days, and it's not pretending, and it's like the Darkness never gave me my monster and I am the old me, and I am good and happy and my immune system didn't send paper planes to my brain and my brain wasn't poisoned and it didn't make me see and hear things and plot against me

and I am well again and I am me, myself, and I laugh and I have fun and I have friends and I am not afraid and I hug my family, throw my arms around my ponies and feel the sun's warm fingers on my neck, and I am fascinated by cobwebs, their intricate patterns and thoughts and those who live in their perfection

and I want it to last, I beg it to last, but it won't because the medicine will stop, and I will be back: the new me will sit in doctors' offices and hospitals and white rooms again as medical professionals talk to me of Autoimmune Encephalitis and PANS and PANDAS or *maybe it's just all in your head* because they won't know and *we've done these tests and what more can you want* and *you are too old* and *you are too young* and *how are you feeling*

and how am I feeling now, because today *is* a good day, and I am my old self, who I was meant to be, but I am scared because I know it's just a good day, not a good week or a good month or a good year, and I want it to be, and it's not fair that these days are dangled in front of me, a glimpse of what a normal person has and I want to be normal, whatever that is

Holly

I pretend I am normal in the front of the horse lorry
watching my pony and her foal on the screen and I am
pretending I am not terrified because my jeans are
touching the seat and there is horse hair on the seat and
my fear does not make sense because I have my own
horses so I should not be scared but I am and I cannot
breathe and I want to be normal for the foal

I pretend I am normal as the drivers talk to me and I am
chatty though I am not a chatty person but I chat and I
talk and I wonder if they see my lurking shame and the
monster inside

I pretend I am normal as the voice in my head gets
louder and it wants me to scream and run but the lorry
is moving so I look at the water under the bridge
instead and imagine I am swimming and free in the lost
days and I know I can pretend I am normal and be
convincing

I pretend I am normal and that I do not see winged
creatures as the drivers tell me my foal is the cutest and
she *is* the cutest and I am proud as I remember how I
helped with her surgery and how her blood soaked me
as the transfusion bag splattered across my face and the
birds were shrieking and I did not react as I wanted and
I did not scream and scream

I pretend I am normal as we reach the equine hospital and I jump out and register us at reception and I am all smiles and it is dark and the dark feeds on my fear and my insanity but I repeat my foal's name over and over because this is for her and she deserves someone who can do this so I pretend I am normal

Yet When I think I Might Have Won, My OCD Monster Still Taunts Me, Because He is Still There, Just Quieter

Oh, you fool!
I'm always here, waiting.
Always here, watching.
You can't dull me forever.
Don't you know that by now?
I'm never leaving you.

Put down that pen, burn that page.
You only need my words,
you just need me.

And I am here.
One good day doesn't mean I've gone for good.
It doesn't mean you've won.
It doesn't mean you're better.

You won't be better.
Not when I'm here.
And my promise to you?
I am never leaving you
for you sustain me.
No matter how hard you try,
how many doctors you see,
how much treatment you have.

I will always be here.
You're mine now,
and friends don't leave.

Alone

The caves are silent
empty
but still I hear them
the voices
muted this time
but still here
thank you
my only company.

Little spiders help me
breathe
because the monster's gone
everyone's gone
and I am bleak
my spongey heart
a wasteland no one wants
plucked
from existence.

Responses When I Seek Help, Again

I don't know why you're calling.
What do you want?
We can't do anything.
You'll just have to wait.
Yes, I know you need those tests.
But I cannot order them.
You need a specialist to request them.
Just wait a few months until you see one.

Why are you calling again?
I told you before.
There's nothing I can do.
Just go to Accident and Emergency.
That's what it's there for.
Oh no, they won't know about this there.
You'll just be wasting your time.
Time and resources.

You, again.
Do you know how much you're costing?
No, I don't believe you.
I haven't heard of this condition before.
None of us have.

Oh, you're back *again.*
Look, I still don't know what I can do.
I don't know who to refer you to.
PANS is too rare.
And really, aren't you too old for this?
What do you want me to do?

It's the Little Things

It's the little things,
the mundane concerns,
that burn and burn
holes in my mind,
holes I fall
into, flooded
with so many spiders,
insects, birds.

And I'm trying to escape,
can't you feel my shouts,
see my screams?

But I can't emerge from the gushing river
and leave behind my shame
because the monster's words are nets
and the nets press
over my burning skin
and I cannot climb
with arms bound so tight.

I cannot kick myself free
from the web
inside my mind.
Too sticky, too strong.

That monster inside me
laughs and laughs
because he has trapped me
with his bait, those little things,
and I'll never be free.

A Thousand Versions of Me

I am here, but I am split in two, three, four:
a thousand versions of myself,
a thousand of me running and hiding,
screaming and crying,
too many sad petals falling
and I trip and fall,
fingers in the mud, badness under my nails
and there is nowhere to go but down.

Don't

No, don't laugh
don't tell me you're OCD
because you think
it's fun, a fad, frivolous
and trendy
don't use it as an adjective

I beg of you
with frozen hands
because you can't see me,
the struggle I'm going through,
how strong I am,
and you belittle me
and thousands of others
who are slaves to their monsters
with your words
just a joke, you meant

but it's not a joke
and I am ashamed
and I am crying and trying to escape
the prison that you jokingly
call yours.

Psycho

The screen flashes; my laptop, my lifeline,
a connection to others, where I have friends,
until the screen is filled with messages,
too many messages with words meant to sting,
and these people don't think it will hurt, not really.
Because it's not in person.

But the wasp thrives after leaving its poison,
and I am a wasteland, watching friends evaporate,
lost in the grid.

I delete the apps from my phone,
but I cannot delete the insults from my memory
those harmful words that carved me out like poison.
And I am marked by them, for anyone new to see.

Psycho. Freak. Headcase.

I hold onto my tears, cradle them close
for they are all I have left. Loyalty is a tough find.

Evict the Monster

Evict the monster and let me live.
Let me breathe and fly and run.

I see the others playing, laughing,
and I want that.

But the others have not got my monster
breathing inside them.

He is mine, the friend he pretended to be,
though when I think about it,
he has never been a friend,
he just told me that he is and that I must not argue.

Teeth and claws that were my own,
but his possession. Biting and biting,
and I am scared.

Searching for Help, Again

5 A.M., how nice your shrill welcome is
hushed calls
and whispers
don't be afraid

my mother
the train
six hours and we're there
aching shoulders and Covent Garden
tighten my coat and stand taller
and so many people
and the Eye
watching me

a friend and his car
and Great Ormond Street hospital
not easy to park

but the specialist works here
my best hope

but I try not to hope
because venom will follow
no point in grabbing the sweetness
when it will be snatched away
I've learnt my lessons

talking and tests and examinations
a starfish on the wall
watching from its picture frame
too many legs and beady eyes

I want to be that starfish
no more red crimson tests
just life in a picture frame
protected behind glass.

If I'd Been Well

It is too much to think of what might have been
and what could've been between us
if I'd been well and normal
to think of the soft life that could've been mine
if my brain wasn't angry and inflamed and under attack

and you're out there
my family and friends
and you're observing me
and so I run
because no matter what I do
you can't see the real me
because the monster forbids it
because I can't be *me* anymore

but I don't want you to see the person I am now
when my brain is hurting
because then the mean insults
will be said in person too
and I won't be able to cope with that

if I'd been well, this would be different
happiness and sunsets and soft words
not silence and sobs and stabs to the back
from whose hand I don't even know

but the world is against me
and I am alone.

A Literal Stab in the Back

The technician stabs the needles into my spine
and hums his song, because he's already told me
he hums while he works. And it is a distraction
but it's not enough.

He hits my nerve: an electric shock bolts my knees
to the table and I think I scream,
and my mother's concerned,
and he says I'm doing well
as he carves out my spine, and I try not to be sick.

Two lots of local anaesthetic. I shouldn't feel this
but I do. Pressure and pain, and he takes the pressure
of my spinal fluid, and my head pounds,
but he says it shouldn't. Not yet.

A little low, he says and my shoulders ache
as I stare at the computer screen while sweat
sticks my arms to the paper towel on the bed,
but my feet are the bravest ice
as he gouges my spinal cord because it's fun.

After, he shows me the needles. Immaculate swords,
too thin, and I think of them piercing my eyeballs.

I wonder if my eyeballs will bleed.

A week, and I am stuck. Lying flat,
Arms like stone. My pain is a heavy song
that won't stop
singing its praise and damage as my nerves shake.

And I want it to stop.

Inside the Centre of the Earth

It will only take twenty minutes.

Invisible needles drill my skull, and I am cold,
lying here, thinking of my coat in the locker outside,
lost and alone, fibres fraying from its blue hems.

I stare at my forehead in the mirror above,
too close. Every pore of my skin is visible,
and my hair follicles, I've never seen them so close
and this doesn't feel real, as the metal vibrates
around me and I feel like I'm inside a drill, a big drill,
and we are diving deep.

But I don't want to go deeper
even though I think it might be safe,
the best place to hide and discover and see truth.

You're doing well.

I see the speaker via the other mirror, but his voice
is in my head and I don't like it
because it shouldn't be here when he is out there
because the voices in my head are supposed
to be just for me.

We're finished your brain.

We're going to start on your spine now.

He laughs and talks with a man and a woman
as his machine reads me on its fortieth minute,

for the time was a lie,
and I imagine the day,
next week, next month, next year,
when answers will arrive,
when doctors will say they can help me,
when they tie up the monster and take him away
to the darkest corners that no one can reach.

The Curse of You, My Self-Doubt

Life is closing, walls shuddering,
and I have nothing, so
I fall from your heart, and fly.

Brighter and brighter and brighter
as I soar, as you follow, laughing and whispering:
You cannot do this.

But I want to be free,
I will be free.
You're not holding me back anymore
with your whispered lies
because I won't let you.

The mountain is ripe,
and we are there. Our battleground.
You and me.
A mirror to my face,
and we are the same.

A smile. A laugh. A whisper.
Fists we cannot see.

Glass shards break as I
climb out of your sticky shadows
into the world.

I watch you fall,
but the sun is too heavy,
my skin is too exposed.
Tiny, tiny fires. Scalding tongues

flicker and fight as I burn.

And I am afraid, but I am free.

A Letter to My Monster

My body is your battleground
my brain the site you sieged
trapping me with your insects and birds
and sharp, sharp voices

but I am fighting your paper planes
and I will keep fighting
because you have proven my strength
even when I am scared and broken
because I am still here
and you have tried to drown me in your rivers
too many times
and suffocate me with your feathers

but you are not strong enough to win the war
to send the last arrow

and they're always the same, your tricks and games
and you tell me your lies and they're always the same
as you gorge yourself on sand to spew out at me
to make me scared

and yes
I am scared
but I am scared and broken and strong
because I am still here and I will keep fighting you.

ACKNOWLEDGEMENTS

Special thanks must go to the following people and groups; Meg Eden, my amazing editor, for helping me work out exactly what it is I want to say with this collection; Isvari Mohan Maranwe and S.E Anderson, for your critiques and feedback; Trish Hopkinson and Emily Stoddard, for your expertise on sequencing these poems and providing me with some truly invaluable resources on the academic side of putting together a poetry collection; everyone in my poetry group, for your support and advice; Janelle Alexander and Megan Eccles, for your encouragement and support; MatYan and Sarah Anderson Designs, for the gorgeous cover art; Molly Phipps, for the ebook formatting; Sherre Vernon and S.E. Anderson, for the blurbs; McKenzie Lynn Tozan, for the marketing and book strategy advice; the PANS PANDAS UK Support Group and the PANDAS Parents' Group, for encouraging me to publish this collection, even though doing so terrifies me.

I also need to thank my family and friends for their support, not only in putting together this collection, but also in making sure doctors listened to me, even when I was ready to give up. Thank you for helping me get better.

RESOURCES

If you need help or advice, please contact your doctor or reach out to one of the following:

Beat, a UK charity offering support and information on eating disorders: **https://www.beateatingdisorders.org.uk/** or call 0808 801 0677

Childline, a confidential service for children and young people: **www.childline.org.uk** or call 0800 1111

The Encephalitis Society: **https://www.encephalitis.info/**

Mind's guide to seeking help for mental health: **https://www.mind.org.uk/media/34633808/seeking-help-for-a-mental-health-problem-2017-web-pdf.pdf**

Mind's advice on self-care for psychosis: **https://www.mind.org.uk/information-support/types-of-mental-health-problems/psychosis/self-care-for-psychosis/#.XekIFZP7QU0**

Mind Infoline: **www.mind.org.uk/information-support/helplines** or call 0300 123 3393 (9am-6pm Monday to Friday) or text 86463

OCD Action: **https://www.ocdaction.org.uk/**

OCD UK: **https://www.ocduk.org/**

PANS PANDAS UK Charity:
https://www.panspandasuk.org/

The PANDAS/PANS/AE Network:
http://pandasnetwork.org/medical-information/

The PANS PANDAS UK Support Group on Facebook:
https://www.facebook.com/groups/189721514954497/

The PANDAS PARENTS Support Group on Facebook:
https://www.facebook.com/groups/pandasparents/

Samaritans, support for people experiencing suicidal thought or distress: **https://www.samaritans.org/** or call free on 116 123.

Samaritans, information on different kinds of support available: **https://www.samaritans.org/how-we-can-help/support-and-information/**

Seeking help for mental health under the NHS: **https://www.nhs.uk/using-the-nhs/nhs-services/mental-health-services/how-to-access-mental-health-services/**

Time to Change, an organization focused on ending mental health discrimination: **https://www.time-to-change.org.uk/**

About the Author

Madeline Dyer lives on a farm in the southwest of England, where she hangs out with her Shetland ponies and writes young adult books—sometimes, at the same time. She holds a BA Honours degree in English from the University of Exeter, and several presses have published her fiction. Madeline has a strong love for anything dystopian, ghostly, or paranormal, and she can frequently be found exploring wild places. At least one notebook is known to follow her wherever she goes.

www.ingramcontent.com/pod-product-compliance
Lightning Source LLC
Chambersburg PA
CBHW030650190726
48286CB00008B/2743
9781912369133